Connective Parenting

A guide to connecting with your child

using the NVR Approach

SARAH FISHER

This book is dedicated to my son
Thank you for all you have taught me

Table of Contents

Acknowledgements

I want to thank those who have supported me on my journey, as I started to use NVR to build a strong, connected relationship with my son, through to training as an NVR Practitioner and helping other families.

Thank you, Michelle Shapiro for your ongoing support and guidance.

Thank you to all the parents I have had the privilege of working with. Sharing your experiences of learning NVR and seeing changes in your families has been inspiring.

Thank you to my family for always being there for me, and Munchkin (my son), as we develop our relationship and become a strong family unit.

To all the professionals using NVR to support families and help parents manage challenging behaviour from their children, whatever their circumstances.

Thank you to those who have supported and encouraged me as I've written this book. Your feedback and guidance has been invaluable.

Introduction

Welcome to *Connective Parenting*, a guide to creating a connected family using Non-Violent Resistance (NVR). It has been written to support families who are using NVR as the basis for their parenting style and is designed to be an easy to read guide book full of tips and ideas.

The book explains what NVR is, the principles underlying it and how they translate into families. It looks at how you can create a strong bond with your child and manage difficult behaviours. NVR is not just about dealing with violence as the name might suggest. It can be used for any form of conflict, however minor. It is also not just about crisis management either; you don't need to wait until you are at crisis point to start using it. That being said there doesn't need to be any conflict before you start using the approach. By using NVR, you will be creating a strong bond that will help to reduce potential future issues.

There are different aspects of NVR that work together like a jigsaw puzzle, each having its own part to play and throughout the book we look at each one in turn. The first three key aspects are: the critical importance of 'looking after yourself' as a parent; 'managing difficult or conflict laden situations' and 'continuing to show your child that you love them' (actions speak louder than words!). These are principles that any parent can (and arguably should) use, at any stage of parenting. It doesn't matter how you became a parent, whether you're a birth parent, an adoptive parent, a step parent, a foster parent or a grandparent, the philosophy of NVR will help you to build, or rebuild, a relationship with your child that is loving and supportive.

Throughout the book the word 'child' has been used. This is for ease of writing only and does not suggest that NVR should only be used with one child. It can and should be used with all the children in a family. It also does not mean to you would only use NVR with a younger child, but with older children (such as adolescents or young adults) also.

What is NVR?

Non-Violent Resistance (NVR) has been used for many years as a way of taking a non-violent, but strong and active stand against aggressive regimes. Mahatma Gandhi and Nelson Mandela both used Non-Violent Resistance very successfully to change seemingly fixed political situations.

This philosophy was adapted by Prof Haim Omer and his doctoral students, for use by parents faced with anger and aggression from their children. It can be used by anyone faced with difficult conflictual situations and/or wanting to build strong, connected relationships, both within a family setting and within work settings.

Within a family setting NVR focusses on developing strong relationships between the parent(s) and child, and uses a child focussed approach. It does not try to change the child through gaining insight or by using consequences or rewards, but uses the personage of the parent and the presence of the parent(s) in the child's life, known in NVR terms as 'Parental Presence', as an alternative. It uses reconciliation gestures to let the child know they are loved, thought about and even understood, and are a means by which the parent can begin to address the child's unmet needs. NVR is about actions not words, particularly early in the process, and so it is more about doing things that show your child you love them, rather than just telling them.

Raising Parental Presence provides the opportunity to change the child's behaviour and your relationship with them. By doing this the parent creates a stronger and more positive internal representation of themselves in the child's mind.

NVR can be used by itself, or alongside other therapies. It takes commitment from the parent(s) and persistent use, but it is very effective. I can personally attest to its effectiveness.

Within adoptive settings NVR is often thought of as an intervention for when things have or are going wrong, however NVR works equally well in the early stages of an adoption when parents are starting to develop their relationship with the child. Early use may well prevent considerable hardships and sorrow later on.

NVR is easy to understand but not always easy to implement and it can feel counter intuitive. It focusses on actions rather than words, whilst focussing on relationships.

The NVR Map

The NVR map shows the different aspects within NVR. Parental Presence is the central element in building or rebuilding the relationship and interacts with the other areas as appropriate for each family.

The aspects at the top of the diagram, 'Looking After Yourself', 'De-escalation' and 'Reconciliation Gestures', are the first key areas of focus to be used by all families, and are where we start the NVR journey. Without actively focusing on these areas, the rest is much harder to do and will not work very well.

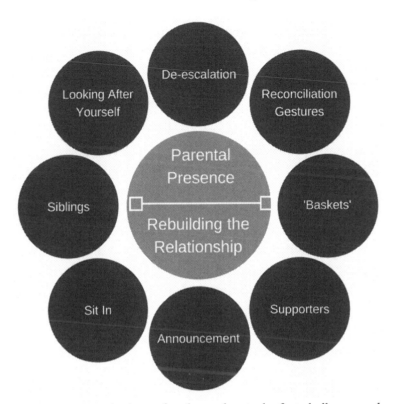

For many parents looking after themselves is the first challenge, and often the hardest. However, doing it makes everything else possible.

This book goes through each aspect on the map enabling you to start using NVR immediately. It takes time to see change, so don't give up if things are not perfect within days. It can take weeks or months for long held behaviours, in both the parent and the child, to change.

Does NVR work with other therapies?

The simple answer is yes. NVR is a way for parents to build or rebuild a strong, connected relationship with their child/ren. A child may still need therapy to support them in dealing with trauma, and the parents might as well. However, when parents practice NVR it has a significant positive impact on how they feel about themselves, their child and life in general.

PACE, Theraplay, DDP and sensory integration are all good ways of developing the relationship between the child and parent. There are many other therapies and ways of relationship-building that can also be used and woven into NVR.

A note of caution. If, as parents, you are working with a number of different therapists at the same time, it is important to ensure they are working together as a team. This helps to ensure you don't receive conflicting advice, or become overwhelmed with the support.

How does NVR support and help families?

NVR can have a significant impact on families, bringing about positive change. It isn't easy though. It takes time, commitment and persistent action from the parents to bring about a change in their relationship with their children. As parents, it is you that has to change the way you react and interact with your child. We cannot force change on others but we can change our interactions with them.

NVR has changed many families' lives for the better. It is used with families in many different circumstances; adoptive families, ones where gang violence is a problem and domestic violence situations, to name a few. The philosophy of NVR is flexible, used within a framework that can be adapted depending on the family's circumstances.

Throughout the book examples are shared of how parents have used NVR to change their family dynamic for the better and I (the author) share my personal experiences as a parent who has used NVR to successfully build a connected relationship with my son. Where other parents' stories are shared, names and details have been changed to protect identities.

NVR can be used with a child of any age, including adult 'children'. The principles are the same we just adapt the way in which they are used.

Parental Presence

What is Parental Presence within NVR? It sounds a bit odd doesn't it? - parental presence. Surely as parents we are present. We are often around our children and in their lives, so that's being present isn't it? In NVR it is a lot more than that. Being present, as in in their lives, is very different to actually being 'Present'. For example, it is possible for a parent to be sitting right next to the child, they are physically present, but in their minds they are a million miles away. In NVR, this parent would not be Present with their child, and the child knows it. In NVR terms it is one of the main goals as you raise both your physical and emotional or felt Presence. It shows them you care.

The intention of this is so that over time they have you in their mind, even when you are out of sight. You are a positive voice in their mind to support them when they feel anxious and to help them feel safe. You are an authority figure, not a boss, who is strong and wise.

When as parents we have lost our Presence we can feel helpless and often this can result in the child feeling unsafe and insecure. They sense our feeling of helplessness and take over control more and more to regain a sense of safety and to help them feel secure. This can result in a vicious cycle of control or more to the point, attempted control by both the parent and child is set up - with both ultimately being miserable.

Parental Presence is a way of providing your child with a safe harbour, or secure base, and being an anchor for them. It is like having a piece of elastic between you both that stretches but never breaks and the child can use it to feel connected to you at all times, hence Connective Parenting.

So how can we build our Presence? Here are some ideas to get you started:

- Sit on the floor with them and play a game
- Curl up on the sofa and watch a TV programme together (one they choose)
- Play a computer game with them, even if you hate computer games
- Go to the park together
- Go for a walk or cycle ride together
- Read a story together
- Do some drawings or paint or make things
- Listen to them more!!!!

What you do isn't the important thing (as long as it's a positive experience), it's that you are spending time with them, really focussing on them and giving them your full attention. This isn't 24 hours a day, that wouldn't be possible, but it is for certain periods of time on a weekly, or daily basis. The focus is on quality of time not quantity of time. So, you need to switch off your phone, or at least don't look at it, forget about the housework or whatever other distractions you have and give your child your full attention. Yes, you may not be doing something that you really enjoy, such as playing computer games, but if that's your child's choice go with it. The feeling they will get from spending time with you will pay dividends in the long run and will change your relationship for the better.

What if they don't want to spend time with me?

This can and does happen, particularly if they aren't used to it or it is associated with past traumas. Think about ways that you can spend time with them that they can cope with and it might only be a few minutes at a time to start with. You can build it up slowly. There is no rush.

Here are some ideas you could try:
- Having dinner together
- Talking to them whilst they are getting a drink or something to eat. Those two minutes could make a lot of difference
- Ask them a question about what they are doing to show you are interested
- Give them a toy they like to play with

Small gestures can slowly build over time as your child learns to accept them. Don't push them into spending time with you - that will only cause resentment. Build it up slowly so that they want to.

Parental Presence is not about changing the child, but how they see you as their parent.

Exercise

Spend 5 minutes thinking about how and when you can spend quality time with your child. Where you have more than one child you need to find time for each of them individually.

If you parent as a couple think about whether you will spend time together with each of your children or separately. Do what works for you and your child. Do make sure you also spend time as a family.

Can I do this quickly?

The simple is answer is probably not. It usually takes time to restore it but it is definitely worth the effort as you see your relationship improve.

Not doing it though can have devastating results on your relationship with your child and result in a downwards spiral, where you are feeling numb, exhausted and generally unable to access real feelings of care for your child - an occurrence being called Blocked Care or Compassion Fatigue. Experiencing Compassion Fatigue is hard and where the next chapter on Looking After Yourself becomes critical as it allows you to find the emotional and physical strength to heal yourself and ultimately your relationship with your child.

Does this really make a difference?

Yes! Parental Presence is one of the first things as a parent I started to do after learning about NVR. I thought I had already been doing it as I built my relationship with my son, which I had, but with some minor tweaks it made a lot of difference to our relationship. As a working parent, it becomes even more important to spend quality time with our children regularly and to build on that and then keep that strong, connected bond. It's often during these times that I have great conversations with my son about things that might be worrying him because he knows he has my time and attention. Many parents who use NVR also say that this is one of the most powerful parts and makes a significant difference to their relationship with their child. Increasing your Parental Presence is one of the key aspects to developing a strong relationship, so doing it is critical.

Reminder:

- This is a cornerstone of NVR
- Spend quality time with your child regularly and give them your undivided attention
- Keep it simple

Looking After Yourself

As a parent we can often 'forget' to look after ourselves. We spend all our time focussed on our family, friends, work colleagues and everyone else that we forget to focus on ourselves sometimes. For us to be able to continually give and support our child we need to look after our own body and mind. When we think of self-care it can be easy to assume it means spending an hour at the gym, or going out with friends and sometimes the thought of finding that time is overwhelming. We immediately think, no I can't do it and so it never happens.

All day every day we are looking after ourselves. We eat, we sleep, we breathe. Taking the time to do those more consciously maybe all that you need to do differently. Take time to taste the food you're eating, enjoy the feeling of the water pouring over you in the shower, go to bed a bit earlier. It's surprising how a little bit more sleep can really change how we feel.

Taking time to look after yourself doesn't need to be something that takes a long time, and shouldn't be seen as another thing you have to try and squeeze into your day. If you're feeling totally exhausted, overwhelmed and don't know where to turn or how to move forwards this is where you need to start. Take a few minutes now, close your eyes and breathe deeply and slowly, in and out 5 times. A small act like this is the start of your journey.

It's something that you can do every day, multiple times if you want to. You will be surprised how a seemingly small act can make such a difference.

Self-care doesn't need to be about spending time alone. For some chatting and laughing with a friend is a great stress release, or dancing round the kitchen listening to music, having fun with your family. All of these things help to release any stress we are holding and allow our bodies to recalibrate.

It is about finding what will work for you and then doing it. Put it in your diary and stick to it. Don't set goals that are impossible to meet, baby steps are great. As with all of NVR it's actions that have the power to change situations.

When we are calmer we react differently to situations. It is easier to stay calm in confrontational situations and we are less likely to overreact, which will have positive benefits for your life. In the next chapter we talk about De-escalation and the importance of staying calm.

The idea of self-care can seem impossible at times. Just getting out of bed and through the day maybe all that you can cope with. When you feel like that, looking after yourself is definitely not a luxury, it's essential, but you need to be realistic about what you can do. Taking 5 deep breaths morning and evening might be 'all' you do, but it will help. At times like this don't put pressure on yourself or feel bad because you're not doing 'enough'.

There is a self-care continuum and we are all on it albeit at different places. We also usually move up and down along the continuum depending on what is happening in our lives, and the amount of self-care we are doing. The key is knowing where you are on it and what you can do at that time to look after yourself.

Survival ---- maintenance ---- wellbeing

In survival mode putting the children in front of the TV for an hour does not make you a bad parent. If it allows you a bit of breathing space and enables you to get a few jobs done or read a book for a bit, then that will help you and enable you to have more energy to parent. That is a good thing, not a bad thing.

In maintenance mode you might meditate for a short time every day, or go for a walk once a week. Whatever works for you to maintain a sense of sanity and support you to stay calm and healthy.

Wellbeing mode is the ultimate goal in some respects. This is where we can go out for the night, or even have a whole day to ourselves. Possibly even a weekend away alone to really recharge our batteries.

For parents in crisis, wellbeing mode, even survival mode, can seem like an impossibility. Just surviving is hard enough. This is why self-care is not a luxury, but a necessity. The only way to get out of crisis mode is to start caring for yourself so that you have the energy to start to change the relationship you have with your child, and ultimately change their behaviour.

Here are two breathing exercises that you can do to help you relax and rebalance your system. Choose one and do it now before you continue reading.

Breathing Exercise 1

Sit in a comfortable chair that supports your back.

Cross your legs at the ankles, right ankle over left.

Cross your arms at the wrists, left wrist over right, resting them in your lap.

Place your tongue on the roof of your mouth.

Close your eyes and take 5 slow deep breaths.

Breathing Exercise 2

Think of a place or phrase that gives you a sense of peace and happiness.

Sit comfortably and close your eyes. Take a deep breath saying your phrase, or thinking about your place as you breathe in. Repeat as many time as needed.

It is not uncommon to feel slightly light headed afterwards. If you are in a stressed state of being, and you don't normally breathe deeply this sudden rush of oxygen is a shock to the body and can bring about the light-headed feeling. It's a sign the exercises are working and much needed. However, if you are worried please seek medical attention.

Understanding Ourselves

Another area of self-care is understanding and knowing ourselves. NVR focuses on the parent changing their reaction to bring about a change in the child's reaction. You cannot force them to change but you can change yourself which will lead to changes in them. As a parent we all know how skilled children are at finding our 'buttons' and pressing them. Those buttons are our triggers. They could be words or actions that cause a particular feeling within us, usually negative, and a resultant behaviour that we may not like. Often that behaviour can cause an escalation of conflict, which is not helpful to either party. In turn that may leave us feeling upset or hurt or angry, both at our own behaviour and at how our child has made us feel which can lead to a feeling of resentment. Taking time to understand our own triggers and changing how we react to them helps us to remain calm and remove some of the negative feelings we have of ourselves and our child.

Exercise

Over the next week or two, notice when you become 'triggered'. What was the trigger, how did it make you feel and how did you react? Notice how quickly the feeling comes and goes. Jot them down and see if there is any pattern, or one underlying trigger.

Don't try and resolve them all at once, but focus on one area first and think about how it makes you feel. How could you change that feeling and your reaction?

The exercise above will be easier for some than others. It is not about ignoring your feelings, but understanding them. Our feelings come from somewhere within us, so understanding that and how to manage them can help us to deal with life's every day stresses and strains and to remain calm when our children press our buttons. It is easy to ignore this exercise thinking that it won't help or you don't need it. However, experience shows it is very worthwhile and makes a difference to how we feel and interact with our children.

It is certainly something that helped me as a parent and parents I work with report it as being a useful exercise.

Remember the positives

When we feel like everything is going wrong that becomes our focus, we forget that good things are also happening. If you focus on the negative you are more like to bring more negatives into your life. When things are tough, seeing any positives can be really hard, but it is possible to see them, you just need to focus on them.

Here are 2 suggestions for how you can do that:
- Have a jar in the kitchen for positives. Write the positive event on a piece of paper and pop it in the jar. It can be used by the whole family and is a great way of remembering positives.
- Use a journal and at night write down 3 positives from your day before your go to sleep. It will help you fall asleep in a more positive frame of mind and sleep better. If you can't remember any positives from the day look back over previous days and remind yourself of all the good things that have happened.

The small, everyday things are also positives. Getting your child to school on time and dressed is a positive. In fact, getting them to school on time, even in their pj's may be a big positive for you. Yes, to many these may not be seen as positives, but for some they are, you've done it.

> ## Reminder:
>
> - Wherever you are on the continuum, do something for you. Whatever is manageable
> - Make sure you do something regularly
> - Know that self-care is an essential not a luxury - it is part of your 'duty' as a parent to take care of yourself, so that you can take care of your child/children

De-escalation

When situations escalate it can be one of the scariest times you might face as a parent. Learning how to De-escalate situations calmly and quickly can be one of the hardest parts of NVR to master. It isn't easy and there's no set way to do it. Every child is different. Every adult is different. Different things will trigger different reactions in each of us, and it is those reactions that we must master as parents and then help our children to master.

To understand De-escalation, we need first to understand the different types of escalation.

Joint escalation is where one person gets angry and then the other responds angrily. These responses become increasingly angry until one or other person explodes.

Giving in escalation is where one person gets angry and the other person starts to back down. The first person gets angrier and angrier until the other person completely backs down and gives them what they want. For  some, giving in may seem to be the easier option, even though they may know it isn't helping. The first person learns that by getting angrier and angrier the other person will eventually give in, so uses this strategy to get what they want every time. It is also quite frightening for a child to feel that much 'in control' of the situation - and that their parent is unable to assist them to stop this escalation.

Both of these situations will be recognisable to many and they happen every day in all walks of life. You may read these and see yourself straight away. Maybe you always give in, it's easier and possibly you feel it's safer if your child is prone to violent outbursts. Maybe you are the type of person who gets angry and responds aggressively. You want to have the last word and feel like you're in control, after all you are the parent and parents are supposed to be in control aren't they? Maybe you swing between these two, at times getting caught up in the one and at other times getting caught up in the other. You know that neither works, but just can't think of or find an alternative.

21

Recognising your own typical reaction to situations is the first step to changing them. Neither of these options is beneficial to building a connected relationship with your child (or anyone for that matter).

So what is De-escalation?

De-escalation is the middle ground between these types of escalation. It's not giving in through pressure, or escalating. It is to allow you, the parent, to self-regulate and be proactive rather than reactive. By becoming proactive you can take back the control of at least yourself in the middle of the situation, and then you will find you have time later, to plan the action you are going to take and help the child learn to regulate themselves.

STRIKE WHEN THE IRON IS COLD!

(an important NVR phrase)

Learning the triggers

Part of de-escalating is knowing your own triggers and your child's, so that you can manage them before they escalate. You manage your triggers first, then your child's. That is why the exercise in the previous chapter, where you identified your triggers, is so important.

Managing escalations gets easier over time as you recognise the triggers in both you and your child. Initially after an escalation you will realise that you became caught up in it. Then you start to realise during the escalation you are getting caught up in it and can catch yourself. Then after a period you can see the escalations coming and are able to act before they start.

How do you de-escalate?

Understanding De-escalation is one thing, but what do you do when meltdowns happen?

Your focus is on ensuring everyone is safe, and then on your own self-regulation, that is it.

You cannot change your child or get them to see sense when they are in the middle of an escalation. Our brains cannot see reason when we are agitated. Keeping yourself calm, is the success.

You may also need to ensure that those around you (and you) are safe, depending on your child's behaviour. In the chapter on Siblings we talk about how you might do this for your other children. For other adults and yourself, you may need to think about removing yourself from the room if it is unsafe for you to stay. For some children though this can cause feelings of abandonment which may make the behaviour worse, so if possible try to stay in the same room.

How you de-escalate will depend on you, your child and the situation. Each one is different and different parents will find different strategies work for them. Here are some ideas:

- Use humour (carefully and only at the right time - but when it can be used it is wonderful)
- Use distraction
- Tell them you are going to stop talking but will stay with them
- Use the communication model outlined in a later chapter

Take these ideas and try them. Play around with using them and find what works for you. Often parents find that different strategies work at different times, so thinking on your feet is often required. This is where the need for self-care is so important. If you are exhausted it is much harder to stay calm, de-escalate and decide how to manage the situation.

A phrase that works well for many parents is 'Zip It'. It's not one you say to your child during a meltdown but to yourself. If in doubt the less you say during an escalation the better.

Deferring your reaction

When the situation has calmed down, and you are ready, you come back to it and address the behaviour.

When the iron is cold (or at least as cool as possible) after an escalation has ended and you feel calm, you can choose when and how to deal with what happened. The action you take is planned and determined by you, allowing you to be proactive rather than reactive, which is more likely in the heat of an escalation. The action you take will depend on your child and what happened. Talking to them about the event and thinking about how they could manage their emotions can work well depending on the age and ability of the child as well as the state of your relationship at that stage. The better the relationship, the more possibility and leeway you will have to talk things through. In the early days of rebuilding the relationship, you might need to use these talks sparingly and carefully; mostly making sure you try to understand what happened for the child, rather than trying to instil insight into them on the impacts of their behaviour. This is not a lecture from you, hoping that the penny will miraculously drop.

Here is an example of how you might escalate a situation. In this example it is an 8 year old boy who will not come off his Xbox and gets very angry very quickly.

Mum: it's time to come off your Xbox now

Child: No

Mum: come off your Xbox now!

Child: No, shut up and go away

Mum: Do as you're told and come off now! (shouting)

Child: No, go away, I'll do what I want (very angry now)

Mum: (tries to grab the controller) get off it now

Child (pulls back and hits mum)

In this example it escalated quickly. Mum got angry because her child wasn't doing as she asked straight away and ultimately was hit. This frustration as a parent is common, particularly when we are tired or worn down.

Here is a way that the situation could have been handled, and de-escalated.

Mum: In 5 minutes your Xbox time will be over

Child: I want longer

Mum: I understand that you want longer, you have 5 minutes more and then we are going to play football together

Child: (ignores parent)

Mum: (5 minutes later) right it's time to come off now and we are going to have some fun together. Off you come.

Child: no, you can't make me

Mum: well, you're right I can't make you, but as your mum I'm telling you to come off now so that we can have fun together.

Child: I'm in the middle of this game I can't stop, I'll lose everything and let my friends down. 5 more minutes

Mum: OK. What are you playing, it looks fun? I'll watch you for 5 minutes, I'd love to see what you're doing

Child: fine. (said in a stroppy voice). Don't talk.

Mum: OK, I'll sit here quietly. (waits a few minutes) 2 more minutes. (after the 2 minutes) OK it's time to come off now. I really enjoyed watching that, you're very good. Right lets go and have some fun together.

At this point, either the child will come off - usually begrudgingly, or will refuse point blank. If they refuse; calmly remind them that they need to come off. As an alternative you could ask to play with them for 5 minutes to break the tension and then they come off. The aim is for a win-win - so don't try and win at the expense of their losing - in the long run, this will not help. It damages the relationship and their willingness to cooperate with you in the future.

If they point blank refuse - do your utmost to remain calm, repeat the requirement and leave it at that. Later, when all is calm again, talk to them about it and agree some rules for moving forward.

Hopefully this example has helped to show de-escalation in action. The aim is to keep everyone calm so sometimes joining in gets the same result and keeps everyone calm. It may appear to be giving in, but it is an active judgement rather than a reactive decision and your child will know that. Ultimately managing the situation like this is easier, quicker and more pleasant than escalating the situation. It also preserves the relationship and gradually improves the willingness on the part of the child to work with you. I know I am repeating this, but it is that important!

De-escalation is an important part of NVR but it is not in itself going to stop meltdowns from happening. It helps you deal with them when they occur. All the other aspects of NVR, that support you in developing a strong and connected relationship with your child, are the parts that will reduce the frequency of the meltdowns and eventually stop them from occurring. It is therefore important that you use all the aspects of NVR not just De-escalation if you want to positively change your relationship with your child.

Reminder:

- Maintaining perspective is invaluable
- Self-regulation is the key to De-escalation
- Don't try and deal with it in the moment
- Defer your response until everyone is calm

The Communication Model

The way we communicate with our children can have a significant impact on our relationship with them, as well as impact on how they feel about themselves.

Hearing what your child has said and acknowledging it, even if you don't necessarily agree with it, is important. It shows your child that you are listening to what they are saying. As adults we know that it feels better when we know we've been heard, even if the other person doesn't agree with us. Being ignored or helped to 'feel better' is not helpful. Being heard is often the important part.

For children who have experienced trauma they may not feel listened to. This is especially the case for children in care, or who have been adopted, they may not feel that adults can be trusted and will usually have been moved around without any discussion or control over what is happening.

This communication model is an invaluable part of the NVR model and can be used as part of De-escalation. It is a powerful way of diffusing an argument.

It is also a good way to build the relationship between the parent and the child, by increasing the Presence of the parent through actively listening to the child. You cannot actively listen if you are not fully engaged in the conversation.

The model also helps to act as self-care for the parent and give them thinking time when they don't know what to say. By repeating the child's words you can reflect them back to them, rather than taking them in yourself.

Verbal communication like this is a great way of problem solving but it can easily be misinterpreted, where what was said is not what was heard. By using this model and repeating back to the child you are checking that you heard correctly and the child knows that you were listening and can correct if you misheard. Where communication is misheard or poor over a period of time the child 'gives up' as they are not being heard. This can cause emotions to be held within them, which is not a good outcome.

Although communication may be difficult to start with, keep going, it will be worth it in the end and make a real difference to your child and your relationship with them.

Here is an example of how the model works:
    Child: Mum I hate you
    Mum: You hate me?
    Child: Yes!

You are feeding back to the child so they know you've heard.

It is a very simple cycle where the child knows that they have been heard. This style of communication can be used in any walk of life.

Once the second person, in this case Mum, knows they have heard correctly they can elaborate and the conversation may look something like this:

    Child: Mum I hate you

    Mum: You hate me?

    Child: Yes!

    Mum: I'm sorry you feel that way, I don't hate you

If the second person has not heard correctly the first person, in this case the child, can correct them.

    Child: Mum I hate you

    Mum: You hate me?

    Child: NO! I said I hate me

    Mum: You hate yourself?

    Child: Yes

    Mum: I'm sorry you feel like that. I don't hate you. Can you tell me more about that feeling? I want to be able to help you.

This method also gives the child an easy way to change what they said without looking bad, which is better for their self-confidence. This can happen when they didn't mean what they said, and it was maybe said out of anger or as a way of communicating something to you.

Some people do find this model hard to use, and feel that it can sound unnatural when used. It is a good idea to practise this first with your partner or a friend before you first use it with you child, so that you feel confident doing so. It is important that you can either adopt a neutral tone, sounding in any way sarcastic or rude will not help the situation; or your tone is reflecting real interest and curiosity about what the child is saying 'Really? - that is important/interesting... please say more!'. It's a model we can all use in all walks of life, so you can practise with anyone and they can learn as well.

It may seem like a small thing, but do practise and use this model, it works well and certainly made a positive impact for my family.

Reminder:

- Communicating helps meet their needs
- Keep your tone neutral or interested
- Feedback or repeat what they said, using their exact words

Rewards and Consequences

Many parents use the idea of consequences and rewards, it's a standard way of parenting. It seems a logical idea, however it teaches the child to do something for an external reward, or that an external consequence will be given for poor behaviour. This is not a connected way of parenting and doesn't help to develop a strong, connected relationship between parent and child. With children who have experienced trauma however, the reward and consequences method of parenting does not work at all, as they do not respond well to it. They do not associate their actions with the consequences and if their self-esteem is low they may not even be bothered. The consequence is simply confirming what they think of themselves.

There is no punishment in NVR

In NVR rewards and consequences as an approach is not advised. Whilst it can work at times, the underlying theme or aim of NVR is to bring about a co-operative relationship between the parent and child. This means that rewards that a child works towards, for example on a reward chart, is not used. However, rewards that are spontaneous and not expected can be used, and can be part of a reconciliation gesture (see next chapter). These gestures can work very well and can help to increase a child's self-esteem. The unexpected nature of them means that children have nothing to work towards, which they could sabotage to ensure they don't achieve it.

There are no enforced consequences or punishments in NVR. Natural consequences are used as there is a direct link and they are not implemented by anyone. For example a natural consequence might be if a child breaks a toy, then the toy is no longer usable. If it can be fixed the child can help fix it, or it needs to go into the bin. An enforced consequence would be the toy being removed for bad behaviour even if the bad behaviour did not involve the toy.

If you have to think of a consequence it probably isn't a natural one

This way of parenting can seem very counter-intuitive but it is very effective. As a parent I changed to using this approach and since implementing it, there has been a definite improvement in behaviour. I have done it alongside using all the other aspects of NVR as well so that we have built a strong, connected relationship at the same time.

The idea of no consequences can to some feel like you are letting the child 'get away with it'. That is not the case. You, as the parent, decide which behaviours you will focus on as part of an exercise in a later chapter. This is part of that, but also a way of helping children to connect their behaviour to a logical consequence. Over time the child realises that certain behaviours are not worth the consequence that comes with it.

It is also linked to the deferred response that we discussed when de-escalating. After an escalation when everyone is calm you can talk to your child about what has happened and ways of stopping it from happening in the future (perhaps using the communication model). This is a powerful way of supporting them to understand and change their behaviour. It isn't easy for a child to have this conversation, so it does need to be done carefully to not shame the child, and whilst it is not a 'punishment' it is a way of the child having to acknowledge their behaviour.

This approach also means that we are less likely to give out a harsh punishment in the middle of an escalation, when we may also be agitated and not thinking straight. For example 'you're grounded for the rest of your life' shouted in rage. We then have to go back and apologise for suggesting something that is very unrealistic. Apologising isn't bad, as it models positive behaviour but it would be easier to just not say it in the first place.

Reminder:

- Only use natural consequences
- Use unexpected rewards

Reconciliation Gestures

Reconciliation Gestures are one of the key aspects of NVR as they help to build or re-build the relationship, which is the central focus. NVR is based on actions rather than words, which is one of the reasons that these gestures are so powerful. These gestures show your child you love them and are unconditional and considered.

They put the parent in a caring position in the eyes of the child and aim to help the child have a positive image of you, the parent, even when you are out of sight.

For the parent they help to increase the mental image you have of your child. This is especially important if your child's behaviour is challenging. Reminding yourself of the positive feelings you have for the child is critically important and can act like a feel good factor for the parent and the child and be a way of showing the child they are loved.

It is not uncommon for Reconciliation Gestures to be rejected, at least at first. If you don't love yourself it can be hard to accept that others love you and that you deserve to be loved. In these situations it is vitally important that the parent carries on giving them and using Gestures that meet the child's unmet needs are most likely to have a positive effect.

At times these gestures can be used to repair, when the parent needs to. For example this may be after a situation where the parent also escalated. By using Gestures like this the parent is modelling to the child how to reconcile and repair.

There are different types of Gestures that you can make.

Initially you might start with small Gestures, these might be:
- a treat
- cooking their favourite meal
- sitting on the sofa watching their favourite TV programme with them

You can then develop Gestures that are deeper and tailored towards meeting the child's unmet needs. For example:
- it could be something that shows them how much they are cared for, like a written note
- a gesture to build their self esteem
- supporting them with a particular area of their development e.g. taking them swimming

The spontaneity of the Gestures is one the powerful aspects of them. The child is not working towards them, it does not depend on them 'being good', they are just given. The feeling you get when you receive an unexpected present is the feeling we want our children to have. This is a big feeling and some may not be able to cope, hence why the Gesture may be rejected. Over time as you use NVR and keep going, their self-esteem will start to improve and they will be able to accept the Gestures, even if they do not entirely believe they are deserved.

It isn't unusual for 'bad' behaviour to follow a Reconciliation Gesture as the child tries to prove to themselves and those around them that they don't deserve to be loved. So be ready for this, should it happen, and keep going with the Gestures.

Reminder:

- Regarless of child's behaviour
- Regardless of how the parent feels towards the child - they are done even when, or perhaps especially when, the parent is feeling negative about the child and their relationship
- Regardless of whether they are accepted or appreciated

Prioritising Your Concerns - the Basket Technique

We all know how hard it is when we try to deal with everything at the same time. Whether that's trying to multitask and complete the household chores or parent your child (or both at the same time!). It's not easy and often results in less being done. The fewer things we focus on at once the more we achieve.

Managing your child's behaviour is exactly the same. If you are trying to deal with every bit of behaviour you don't like at the same time, it is exhausting and often unfruitful and will result in more problems. In NVR one of the aspects focuses on prioritising your concerns, often called 'Baskets' it is effectively helping you as the parent to 'pick your battles'!

There are 3 baskets to help you prioritise:

Low priority behaviours

Middle priority behaviours

Top priority behaviours

The small basket is your priority basket. In this one you put no more than 2 behaviours that you want to deal with. These are the things that absolutely must change/stop. If you are experiencing violence from your child, then that will nearly always go in the top basket. If not, then prioritise what you feel is the worst behaviour.

The middle basket is for those things that you can negotiate on. For example that might be bad language. You are not going to totally ignore these behaviours but you will think about when you choose to deal with them.

The large basket is for everything else. It is for all the behaviours that you are going to ignore for now. So that might be things like table manners. They may be things that you find really annoying, but for now you are not going to deal with them. I know there will be many people reading that thinking, 'no way! I'm cannot let them get away with those behaviours'. That's a natural response and one I had when I first did this. It feels like you are letting them get away with things and instinctively that feels wrong. The intention though is to release some of the pressure from you and allow you to focus on the top priority behaviour only. Many parents who do this find that over time, not only does the top priority behaviour go, but other behaviours improve as well even though they haven't been focused on. I liken it a bit to being nagged. If you are constantly being nagged it can affect how you feel about yourself and make you less likely to do the thing you are being nagged about. When the nagging stops you start to feel better and may naturally start changing your behaviours.

Exercise:

Draw the 3 baskets on a piece of paper.

Get a packet of sticky notes (or tear up a piece of paper) and on each one write down a behaviour that you find annoying and or is unacceptable. Break down the behaviours, don't just write 'bad behaviour', that could break down to 'swearing', 'violence', 'defiance' etc. on all different notes.

Once you have done this, decide which basket each behaviour will go in, remembering that the largest basket should be the fullest.

Once you've done the exercise, keep it somewhere as a reminder. You can revisit it whenever you need to and once the top priority behaviours have subsided you can review your baskets and decide what is the new top priority. It isn't uncommon to find that some of the other behaviours have decreased as well.

In the Looking After Yourself chapter we talked about having a 'positives' jar or journal to remind yourself of the positives. A positive basket or bag is a way of remembering the positives about your child. It works on the same lines as the journal but focuses on your child's positive attributes and skills. You might like to start one now writing down all the positives about your child, for example they have a wonderful sense of humour, or a nice smile. Over time you can review the bag and add in more positives as they grow and develop. When you're having a bad day read the notes in the bag and remind yourself of the positives.

Reminder:

- Choose to not address the behaviours in the big basket - 'let it go'
- Focus on your small basket behaviours
- Be consistent as parents and agree what is in each basket

Supporters

Having people around you to help and support you is really important. The saying **'it takes a village to raise a child'** is very true.

Many parents don't want to ask for help, they see it as a weakness and feel that they have failed if they can't manage it themselves. This isn't true.

Asking for help is a strength

You can parent without support, and many do, but why not ask for help when you need it and make it a bit easier?

In NVR supporters are used in different ways.
- As mediators
- As an ear when you need someone to talk to
- As a witness

They can be for both the child and the parents, and siblings may also benefit from having their own supporters.

Having the right type of supporters is also important. You need people who will genuinely support you, who understand what you are trying to achieve and will back you up when needed. You don't need people who don't understand or agree with your approach as this can be very undermining and ultimately may cause more damage to your relationship with your child.

Who could you ask?

Anyone! That's the short answer. Be inventive about who you can ask, they might be in your immediate or more extended network.

Here are some ideas:

If you're part of an NVR Support Group ask parents there and support each other.

How to ask supporters for their help

Think carefully about who you want to ask. It may be family, friends, neighbours, professionals such as therapists, school staff, or a combination. Each person can have a different role and one that you feel they will be able to do. For example a friend may be a great listening ear when you need to let off a bit of steam; a neighbour may make a great witness and be able to pop in quickly if needed.

Once you have decided on a person and the role you would like them to have, it's time to ask them for help. If you are the sort of person who never asks for help, this part may not come easy. Remember that most people are only too glad to help when needed - provided they know what is being asked of them and it is not too overwhelming.

If you're worried about asking the same people too much, have a larger pool of supporters then rotate asking them. It's a great way of not feeling like you're asking too much of one person.

When you're talking to them, be clear what it is you need their support for and how you would like them to help you. This way, they understand what you need and if they genuinely don't feel they can do that they are more likely to say so. You could give them some notes if that's easier, or website links (see useful links at the back of the book) or a copy of this book, so that they can find out more about NVR and how you are choosing to parent. It's important that you explain what you need them to do, ie if you call them round to witness a situation do you want them to intervene or just stand back and watch? Where do you want them to be in the room or house?

Giving all of this information makes it easier for the person supporting you, they will feel more comfortable and when it happens and they are needed they will know what to do. Although the reality of a situation may be very different from their expectation, particularly if they are witnessing a situation for the first time.

Reminder:

- Don't be afraid of asking for help
- Be clear what you would like your supporters to do
- Explain to them why you are parenting the way you do

Siblings

When the behaviour of one child is hard to manage it can be easy to focus all our energies on that child, sometimes to the detriment of the others.

As part of implementing NVR, siblings need to be considered and all of the aspects can be used for all children in the household.

Showing your child you love them, is something all parents want to do, so do Reconciliation Gestures for all of your children. You can personalise them to each child to meet their own needs and it shows you know them each as individuals and love them equally.

Managing difficult behaviour in the same way is also important, so that the siblings do not feel like anyone 'gets away with it'. If you can explain the principles of NVR to them and make sure that they have supporters for themselves.

It isn't unusual for children to feel scared, resentful or unhappy if their sibling's behaviour is difficult. Take time to talk to them and try to reassure them. You may also want to put a plan in place so that they have somewhere to go if a sibling starts being violent or aggressive, for example a safe place to 'hide'.

Younger children can also copy the behaviour of older children, particularly if they feel unsafe and insecure themselves, or they see their older sibling getting what they want from their behaviour (whether or not that is actually happening). By using NVR with all your children you can reduce the likelihood of this happening, or stop it from starting.

By using NVR as a way of parenting all of your children they will see that they are being treated in the same way, and will know that they are loved and cherished for who they are.

Reminder:

- Use the NVR principles with all of your children
- Be persistent - you'll have good days and not so good days. The key is to keep going

The Self Announcement

As parents, we may do things that we regret, that may hurt ourselves or our child. A Self Announcement is a letter to ourselves and is an important part of NVR.

In the letter, you are forgiving yourself for what it is you feel you have done wrong. That might be shouting at your child, harshly punishing them, or not being nurturing enough. It will be different for everyone.

The key thing is to be honest with yourself. No-one else will see the letter.

Writing the letter is a form of self-care where you are releasing some of the negativity inside you and allowing positive feelings to replace it.

The letter is written like a sandwich, with the two slices of bread being the positive information and the filling the thing you want to forgive yourself for.

The start of the letter is your top slice of bread and where you say what you like about yourself. For example, I'm sensitive, caring and funny.

The filling is where you'll say what it is you want to forgive yourself for and/or for what you want to change/stop doing. For example, I

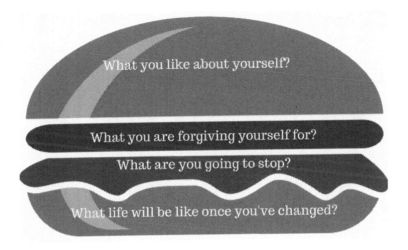

What you like about yourself?

What you are forgiving yourself for?

What are you going to stop?

What life will be like once you've changed?

forgive myself for shouting at my children when I'm angry and will stop doing it. I will find a different way of dealing with my anger and look after myself so that I can regulate my feelings more easily.

The bottom slice of bread is where you write about what life will be like once you have stopped. For example, I'm looking forward to when I'm not shouting at the children and am remaining calmer.

Reminder:

- Be honest with yourself
- Take the time to write the letter, see it as self-care

Acts of Resistance - Parental Disobedience

In the following chapters we look at how as parents we can change the status quo and show our child we are not going to give in. For some families these acts will not be needed as the implementation of the aspects up to this point, is enough to change the behaviour at home significantly. For others, particularly those with older children or where the behaviour is more embedded these acts may be needed.

This is a way of the parents showing that they have drawn a line in the sand and are intent on keeping it there. They will do everything in their power to help their child and will not stop being there for them whatever happens.

All of the acts discussed in the coming chapters focus on the top priority behaviours that are in the small basket. That is where as parents all your effort is focused.

Parental disobedience is where we are not doing as the child expects or wants us to do. For example they want us to give in every time they have a meltdown so that they are in control. By De-escalating we are taking that control away and not doing as the child wishes in that moment. This can and should be done during every escalation.

As parents, we can do little acts where we do not comply with orders or demands. For example; when the child demands something you make the child wait until you have finished the task you were doing or have popped to the loo. You are not asking them to wait a long time, maybe 5 minutes, but the act of not immediately doing as requested raises that parent's Presence.

It is important though that parents think about how and when they use this type of disobedience. Using it all the time is not right as it gives the child a negative impression that they are not as important as the task the parent is performing. They should also be used very carefully, if at all, at the start of the relationship when it is important that the child learns the parent is there for them.

It is also only used for non-priority behaviours, so behaviours in the large basket, not the small one.

These small acts of resistance can help you, as the parent, to feel like you are in control again, however ensure that they don't become ways of acting against the child in a negative way.

Reminder:

- Use these acts sparingly
- Only use them for low priority behaviours
- Do not use them negatively against your child

The Announcement

This is a formal part of NVR and focusses on the top priority behaviour, the one in the small basket. It is a formal statement to the child, from the parents, about that behaviour.

It is not about shaming the child or being harsh, but a 'love letter' to the child telling them about how you will be changing your parenting in a firm, clear and caring way.

The Announcement takes the form of a letter which usually parents read out to their child, although it can be emailed or sent via text.

How do you write an Announcement?

It has the same format as a Self Announcement in that you write it like a sandwich, but there is a bit more filling.

The top slice of bread is all the positives about your child. You can include things about your relationship, improvements in behaviour and the positive things in their personality, for example their humour or caring nature.

You then move on to the filling in the sandwich which has several parts.

- You start with an apology from you for your own past errors and say that you will do all you can to stop it from happening again. This is similar to your Self Announcement.
- You then introduce the priority behaviour that you are focussing on and the effect it is having on the family. For example 'When you are angry you hit and kick mummy which is painful and upsets everyone. This is something that needs to stop.'
- You confirm that you will do everything you can to support your child and stop the behaviour. 'As your parents we will do everything we can to help you stop doing this.'
- The last part of the filling is telling your child you will not keep it silent anymore and will be asking for help from others who love and care about you all. Breaking the silence and getting support is a very powerful way of stopping the violence.

The bottom slice of bread is where you tell your child you love them and want the best for them. You might say things like 'we want to be able to have fun together' and or 'we want you to have a good and happy life'.

The language you use needs to be right for your child, for example use 'hit' or 'kick' if they wouldn't understand 'violence' and if they are non-verbal use pictures.

Read the Announcement to yourself out loud and see how it sounds. Have someone read it to you and see how it feels. It should be clear and come from a place of love and support, not sound aggressive and angry. You are addressing the behaviour because you must and you are doing that because you care for them. That is the message you want the child to hear.

You may need to write and re-write the Announcement several times until it feels and sounds right.

How do you deliver an Announcement?

Preparation is key!

You need to carefully plan for the Announcement if it is to have the desired effect. Here are the steps to take when preparing:

- Read and re-read the Announcement until you are happy with how it is written.
- Practice reading it, until it feels comfortable.
- Role play how you will deliver the Announcement, practising who will sit where, who will read it.
- Think about who should be there when you deliver it, you may want a supporter in the house, if not in the room with you.

It can also be beneficial to give the child a Reconciliation Gesture at the same time, so plan and think about what you could do, and have it ready.

When you are ready deliver the Announcement to your child. Don't worry if it isn't 'perfect' or doesn't seem to have been 'successful'. The whole act of delivering the Announcement helps to empower you, as parents, and will change the dynamic between you and your child even if it isn't evident.

Once you've started keep going, even if you don't think they are listening.

Delivering an Announcement isn't easy but it is effective so be brave and do it if you need to.

What next?

Give a copy of the Announcement to your child. You could put it up on a wall somewhere or leave it on their bed with a Reconciliation Gesture.

You will only deliver the Announcement once for each top priority behaviour and you don't get into a discussion about what you wrote in it.

In the next chapter we talk about the NVR 'Sit in', which follows an Announcement if their behaviour continues.

Reminder:

- Focus on your top priority behaviour
- Preparation is key!
- Only deliver it once

The 'Sit in'

In NVR the 'Sit in' is considered by some to be the BIG GUNS of NVR and takes place after an Announcement has been delivered. It is used if the priority behaviour has reoccurred after the Announcement.

Not all practitioners use it though and not all families will get to the stage where they need to use it. But if that extra step is needed, then the Sit-in is invaluable and should not be shied away from.

What is it?

The 'Sit in' is effectively a way of parent's actively protesting against their child's behaviour. It is a very simple, yet effective technique and involves the parents literally 'sitting in' with the child. Usually it takes place in the child's room and the parents will briefly explain why they are there and ask the child for a solution to the problematic behaviour. The parents then sit mostly in silence.

Why use it?

It is a way of raising Parental Presence and reinforcing the message delivered during the Announcement. It shows to your child that as parents you are serious about helping them to address and change their behaviour and that you will not give up. You will find a way forward with them. It is also an important holding and thinking space created by the parents for the child but also for the parents themselves.

When do you do it?

- After a reoccurrence of a priority behaviour.
- When things are calm - When the iron is cold, or at least cool.
- When you have had time to plan what you will do, who will be there and how you will do it.

How do you do it?

It is important that you plan how the 'Sit in' will work and who will be there.

Think about whether you would like supporters in the house. They don't need to be in the room, they could remain downstairs and be there if needed.

The 'Sit in' is usually led by the parent who is most disempowered by the behaviour you are targeting. They may be the least present parent and or the one who is attacked the most. The lead parent is the one who will introduce why the parents are there. For example they may say something like:

'We told you that being violent towards me
must stop.
You hit and kicked me yesterday.
This needs to stop.
Do you have any ideas on how you could stop this?'

Both parents then sit in silence.

During the Sit in your child may try and engage you in conversation, or behaviour in a way that is clearly trying to engage you. Where possible avoid engaging. It may be necessary to repeat why you are there.

You want to have somewhere to sit, so depending on the room you may need to take chairs in with you. It is best NOT to sit on the floor, it makes you too vulnerable, and it is best not to sit in front of the door as this may seem threatening.

How do you end a 'Sit in'?

There are 3 ways in which a 'Sit in' can end.
1. The allocated time us up
   a. For a 'normal' functioning adolescent that is about 1 hour
   b. For a child between 9 and 12 about ½ an hour
   c. The length of time reduces for younger children and those with neuro-developmental difficulties
   d. For children under 5 a 'time in' is an effective solution
2. Your child is violent and it becomes unsafe
   a. Leave the 'Sit in' telling your child that the problem is still there and you need to think about how to resolve it
   b. Ensure that you include supporters for the next 'Sit in' as they are generally a deterrent to violence
   c. Plan the next 'Sit in' with even more care
3. Your child comes up with a solution
   a. A solution that is even remotely workable is accepted first time it is offered. It still shows that thinking has begun, and it allows the 'Sit in' to end (unless it is totally ridiculous)

b. You can explore the idea a little and say something like, 'that may work, let's try it'

c. You can then leave

What next?

If the behaviour re-occurs you do another 'Sit in', and if needed another until the behaviour stops, or you can see the child is making a real effort to stop it, e.g. they stop themselves mid behaviour and are learning to self-regulate.

Reminder:

- The 'Sit in' is reasserting your Parental Presence and reinforcing the Announcement
- It is planned and controlled and done when calm
- It is about finding a way forward together

The Campaign of Concern

This is a way of showing your child how much you care about them and are worried about them. It is particularly effective with older children as you are staying connected to them after an escalation, when they are more likely to try and disconnect and potentially engage in more problematic behaviour.

By using this technique, you are raising your Parental Presence to minimise any further disconnection and deter further escalation.

This is not about punishing your child and also helps you, as the parent, to reconnect to your child when your instinct maybe to chuck them out and lock the door.

If your child goes out and you are worried, maybe they haven't returned by the agreed time or are not responding to your text messages, you use your supporters and their friends to check they are OK.

To do this you need to collect their friend's mobile numbers and maybe their friend's parents contact details. You need to ask the friends if they would be willing to share their contact details. Explain the situation and hopefully they will be willing to help. Many parents would be willing to exchange contact details, as it helps them as well.

Connective Parenting

So how do you do it?

If your child isn't responding to you start to text their friends and see if you can find out where your child is. Explain that you are worried about them and just want to check they are OK. As you start texting the friends you will hopefully get a response and be able to find out where your child is. The impact of this is that often the friends will start getting frustrated and ask your child to respond. It can lead them to tell your child they are lucky that their parents care so much. This is the response one family got from their daughter's friends when they used this approach. Over time their daughter acknowledged that and started to be more responsive to her parent's requests.

Another step you can take is going to the places where you think your child might be and just 'hanging out' there. You need to be careful and plan what you are going to do, to ensure you are safe and that it is a positive action. However, it can be a powerful action and shows your child you will not give up on them.

Your child may do everything in their power to stop your actions having the desired effect, so be aware of that and keep going.

For these actions to be successful you need to:
- Keep calm
- Be clear what you expect, e.g. they should come home
- Do not escalate and avoid arguments as much as possible
- De-escalate and don't be drawn in
- Don't try to overpower your child. Just be there and raise your Parental Presence

The intention of these actions is to resist your child's attempts at detaching from you, not necessarily to bring them home. You want them to know you are there for them and there will be no punishment for their actions.

Bringing it all together

Throughout this book, you've learnt about the different aspects of NVR and how they work together to support you in building a connected relationship with your child and your family as a whole.

If you're feeling overwhelmed with life, then you need to start with Looking After Yourself and do nothing else. Don't try and be a 'perfect' parent (I don't think they exist anyway), or implement all the strategies we've talked about straight away. If you feel like you're at the survival end of the self-care spectrum, you need to focus on you and only you right now. I'm not saying forget about your children, of course not, just don't try and be super parent and don't feel guilty about it either. Once you start to feel a little less overwhelmed then think about introducing some Reconciliation Gestures, they are a great way to reconnect with your child. While you're doing that start to notice how you are when your child starts a meltdown and start working on De-escalation.

It is not a race, go at your pace and start implementing the different aspects when you are able. Remember if you focus on the key three aspects (Looking After Yourself, De-escalation and Reconciliation Gestures) you will start to see glimmers of light at the end of the tunnel. The other aspects help you to get there and like a jigsaw puzzle all the pieces together make the picture.

NVR will help you to feel empowered as a parent and to resume your natural role of parent. It will not be easy, or quick, but it will work. I can personally attest to its effectiveness, as can may other parents.

Reminder:

- Be persistent
- Actions are more important than words
- Keep going, even if it's gone wrong
- Look After Yourself
- Focus on the top priority behaviour in the small basket

Useful Links

www.sarahpfisher.com

The website includes resources and information about NVR, as well as information about training courses

www.nvr-practitioners-consortium.com

The NVR Practitioners Consortium is a social enterprise that provides a list of trained practitioners and courses for parents across the UK. It also provides ongoing training for NVR Practitioners, as well as information about training for professionals.

Printed in Poland
by Amazon Fulfillment
Poland Sp. z o.o., Wrocław